Turtles for Beginners

ALINA DARIA

Copyright © 2023 Alina Daria

All rights reserved.

ISBN: 9798376668535

Contents

Introduction 7

Popular Species 12

Individual husbandry or group husbandry 28

Buying the Turtles 35

The Turtle Home 41

The Diet 53

Brumation 66

Common Diseases 74

Frequently Asked Questions 99

Legal Notice 109

Room for Notes 113

Introduction

There are over 250 species of turtles, many of which are aquatic. It is not easy to determine the exact number of aquatic turtle species, as new species are discovered regularly and some species are recorded and listed differently in different sources. However, it is estimated that there are about fifty to sixty species of freshwater turtles worldwide; this number serves as a rough guide.

We humans have kept aquatic turtles as pets for several centuries. The exact date when turtles became popular as pets is not known, but turtles have long been kept as pets in various cultures around the world.

In China, for example, turtles have been kept as pets for over 2,000 years and are still considered symbols of longevity and good fortune. In the United States of America, the red-cheeked ornamental turtle became popular as a pet in the mid-20th century. This species is still one of the most commonly kept turtle species today, as it is in France, the United Kingdom and also in Germany.

Given the increasing popularity of turtles as pets, it is important for potential owners to know the specific needs and requirements of this species, as well as the responsibilities associated with keeping a turtle as a pet. Turtles, or all pets, respectively, enrich life immensely, are a great hobby, and many of us view our animals as family members. Therefore, it is important to be well prepared before taking responsibility for other living creatures. By purchasing this book, you have already taken the first step!

Aquatic turtles are cold-blooded animals, also known as ectotherms. This means that their body temperature is regulated by the temperature of their environment - unlike us humans and other mammals. The temperature of the body of ectothermic animals is not influenced by their metabolism, but depends entirely on the temperature of their environment. They rely on external heat sources such as the sun or warm water to regulate their body temperature. They usually become lethargic or less active when temperatures are too low. Reptiles and amphibians are cold-blooded animals - and our aquatic turtles are among the reptiles.

Aquatic turtles are growing in popularity and steadily moving into more living rooms or gardens. There are probably several million people worldwide who own aquatic turtles. Whether land turtles or water turtles are more popular as pets is difficult to determine, as this can vary regionally and also depends on availability and care requirements. With land turtles, all sizes are popular, both the small species and the larger ones - for example, the Sulcata land turtle or spurred tortoise can reach a dorsal carapace length of a full eighty centimeters (31 inches) and a weight of more than eighty kilograms (176 pounds). Therefore, while it is not suitable for every household, keepers with a very large garden can also keep this species well outdoors. For aquatic turtles, we are limited to much smaller species, which we will take a closer look at in the following capital, as they naturally rely on plenty of water for swimming.

Turtles have populated our earth for millions of years and existed even before the dinosaurs. Over time, of course, new species evolved and others died or become extinct. Commonly, turtles are considered slow animals, which is correct - however, aquatic turtles can swim much faster than they can walk! Some species even swim faster than us humans. This is another reason why it is so important that we provide enough water area for our aquatic turtles, because this way they can have a nice romp.

Popular Species

For simplicity, we will refer to "aquatic turtles" in this book, but these are often equated with terrapins and to simplify the language we will focus on the term "aquatic turtles" as a generic term. There are several hundred different species, but not all are suitable for keeping at home as pets.

Therefore, we will now take a closer look at some particularly popular species - although it must be mentioned that this list is not exhaustive and there are, of course, other species that are kept by people in terraristics. In order not to go beyond the scope of this book, we will concentrate on widespread, particularly popular species in the following.

1.

Painted Turtles

Scientific name: Chrysemys picta

The Painted Turtle Chrysemys picta is the only species of the genus Painted Turtles. The genus name is of course Chrysemys. Genera like this, which have only one species, are called "monotypic".

In Central Europe the Painted Turtle is mainly known as a terrarium animal, in the wild it is mainly found in North America. Their natural habitat is ponds and rivers.

Painted Turtles reach a size of about 12 to 25 centimeters (5-10 inches). The subspecies Chrysemys picta doralis (southern subspecies) remains particularly small at 10 to 15 centimeters

(4-6 inches), making it well suited for keepers who don't have too much space available.

An aquarium measuring 120 cm x 50 cm x 50 cm (47x20x20 inches) is suitable for two Painted Turtles. If more are added, at least 20% more space should be offered per animal. Of course, these are only the minimum dimensions, which should not be fallen short of under any circumstances. More space is of course always great.

The aquarium should have a temperature of 22-30°C (72-86°F) and under the heat lamp it should be about 35°C (95°F). In the wild, Painted Turtles feed mainly on worms, aquatic insects, snails and aquatic plants.

Chrysemys picta - By Bernell MacDonald

2.

Yellow-Bellied Slider

Scientific name: Trachemys scripta scripta

Yellow-bellied sliders have their original home in the southern part of the United States of America as well as in Mexico. However, since they have been released several times, they can now be found in the wild in Europe, for example.

They live in rivers, ponds, swamps as well as waterways and can reach a size of up to 25 centimeters (10 inches).

Two ornamental turtles should have at least 150 cm x 50 cm x 50 cm (60x20x20 inches) in the aquarium - more space is of course always welcome. At least 20% more space should be offered per additional animal.

Jewel turtles are comfortable at temperatures between 22°C and 30°C (72-86°F). Under the heat lamp it should be about 35°C (95°F). The air temperature should be a few degrees above the water temperature and a humidity of at least 75% is desirable.

Water depth should be at least 12 inches (30 centimeters).

Juveniles of this species feed only on animal food. As adults they then become omnivores. In the wild, they feed primarily on worms, snails, aquatic insects and aquatic plants.

Trachemys scripta by Svetlana Zoosnow

3.

Red-Eared Slider, Red-Eared Terrapin

Scientific name: Trachemys scripta elegans

See number 2.

4.

European Pond Turtle, European Pond Terrapin

Scientific name: Emys orbicularis

The European Pond Turtle has its home, as the name already suggests, mainly in countries like France, Spain, Southern Germany, Northern Italy, Poland - but also for example in Turkey, Iran, Morocco as well as Algeria. They live there in rivers, lakes and wetlands.

This species is diurnal and reaches a maximum size of 25 centimeters (10 inches). It also feeds omnivorously, consuming both plants and animal foods such as insects and worms.

The dorsal carapace is smooth, somewhat convex, and blackish with small yellow spots as well as stripes. The ventral carapace of this species, which has transverse hinges and can be partially closed, is yellowish with a dark spotted pattern. The head, legs and tail are black with yellow spots and stripes.

The male has a long tail as well as a white iris; in the female, the tail is short and the iris is yellow in color.

The European Pond Turtle is most comfortable at temperatures between 18°C and 25°C (64-77°F).

Emys orbicularis by Onkel Ramirez by Svetlana Zoosnow

5.

Spotted Turtle

Scientific name: Clemmys guttata

Spotted Turtles have their natural home in North America, and they are a fairly small-bodied species. They reach a size of about 10 to 13 centimeters (4-5 inches), but can grow up to 15 centimeters (6 inches) long. Despite being so small, this species can live to be quite old. Specimens are known to have lived to be over one hundred years old. However, it is more normal for them to live around fifty years.

The carapace of this species is black with yellow and orange spots. The lower carapace (plastron) is also black and has yellow and orange markings. On the carapace sometimes even more than a hundred spots can be found; this is a little different for each turtle.

The rest of the body, i.e. the head, the tail and the legs, is also black and yellowish stripes and/or spots can also be found here.

The females of this species have a reddish chin when fully grown, whereas the males have a black chin. As a rule, the tail of the males is also thicker and longer than the tail of the females.

6.

Common Musk Turtle, Eastern Musk Turtle, Stinkpot Turtle

Scientific name: Sternotherus odoratus

The Common Musk Turtle is native to the southern part of the United States, where it is particularly fond of tropical swamps, slow-moving rivers, and also lakes.

It lives about thirty to fifty years and reaches a length of seven to thirteen centimeters (3-5 inches) - thus it belongs to the smaller turtle species. On average, it grows ten centimeters (4 inches) long and reaches a weight of just under 250 grams (0.5 pounds). It is also known as the garlic mud turtle because it emits an unpleasant odor when in a threatening situation. The odor is said to repel predators and is reminiscent of the smell of garlic.

The aquarium should have the minimum dimensions of half a square meter by half a meter high (20 inches) and the water should be about 77°F (25°C).

Under the heat lamp it should be about 35°C (95°F).

7.

Red-Bellied Short-Necked Turtle, Pink-Bellied Side-Necked Turtle, Jardine River Turtle

Scientific name: Emydura subglobosa

This species formerly carried the scientific name Emydura albertisii and is now called Emydura subglobosa. It reaches a maximum size of 28 centimeters (11 inches) and is native to Cape York, southern New Guinea and northern Australia - hence it is sometimes called the Australian River Turtle. There it lives in rivers, tributaries, ponds, lagoons, lakes and coastal swamps. It feeds mainly on animal food (mainly insects), but also on some plant life.

The upper carapace of this species is light brown or dark brown, while the ventral shield is orange-yellow to reddish in color.

Usually juveniles have a gray marking in the middle of the ventral side, but this disappears with age.

Red-Bellied Short-Necked Turtles live mostly in the water and usually only come ashore when they want to lay eggs or sunbathe for a while. Therefore, they are very good swimmers. They are most comfortable at temperatures between 22°C and 28°C (72-82°F). They usually live up to thirty years.

Trachemys scripta by Sergio Cerrato

Individual husbandry or group husbandry

There are pets that should definitely be kept in groups and those that are absolute loners. Here, one orients oneself to the way the respective animal species lives in the wild in order to provide the animal with a species-appropriate life. For example, guinea pigs are pack animals, while the vast majority of hamsters are solitary animals.

In the case of turtles, however, this question is not quite so easy to answer and for this reason there is still much debate as to whether aquatic turtles should be kept alone or in groups. This is because aquatic turtle can be solitary or live in a group depending on the species. Not all aquatic turtles are the same - there are many different species from many different regions of the world.

Therefore, it is always advisable to orientate yourself on how the respective species lives in the wild.

In addition, animals also have their own personalities. This depends not only on the sex, but also on the character. There are animals that are more dominant than others, and animals that are more shy. It also happens that animals are sympathetic or less sympathetic to each other.

Land turtles are generally considered to be contact animals, while it is a little more complex with aquatic turtles. This makes for frequent discussion in the community, as when kept singly, it is often criticized that the turtle never crosses paths with another turtle (as in nature).

On the other hand, with group housing, it is often criticized that some turtles (depending on the species) do not form solid groups. Therefore, many keepers try to find a compromise by keeping several turtles together, but in such a large area that the turtles can always get out of each other's way and have enough privacy, but can "meet" if they wish.

Some turtles are quite social and like to interact with other turtles or even humans. Others, however, prefer to be alone and can become stressed by too much contact. It is essential to understand and consider the needs of each turtle in order to create a species-appropriate environment for them.

The natural lifestyles of some species in the wild:

Chrysemys picta - Lives in larger groups in the wild. For example, likes to be kept in groups of four to five females, taking care to ensure that individuals get along. The different subspecies can theoretically be kept together, but Chrysemys picta dorsalis requires different temperatures than the other subspecies.

Trachemys scripta scripta and Trachemys scripta elegans - In nature, lives in large groups that like to bask together.

Emys orbicularis - Usually lives in smaller groups in the wild and are considered semi-social.

Clemmys guttata - Are also semi-social and live in smaller groups in the wild.

Sternotherus odoratus - Lives mostly as solitary in the wild and avoids larger groups compared to other species. Although this species tends to be solitary and is often encountered alone, it is possible for several turtles to bask together and then go their separate ways.

Emydura subglobosa - In the wild, sometimes lives alone, sometimes in groups, though not in groups as large as the species listed at the beginning. They also like to bask with other individuals, but require a lot of privacy and like to go their own way. If they are kept in groups, it is especially important with this species to make sure there are plenty of places to retreat.

Other aquatic turtles that are usually solitary in their natural habitat include the Kinosternidae, Glyptemys, and Terrapene.

In addition, the following points are equally important:

- Aquatic turtles should not be kept with other species.

- Aquatic turtles should (if at all) only live in groups of the same species, as different species also have different requirements in terms of temperature, humidity, and the like. In addition, different species often exhibit different behaviors.

- Young animals should not be kept together with adults. Group housing often works better with young animals and can become problematic later if some animals become particularly dominant. However, this also depends on the individual character.

- A single turtle already needs a lot of space; several turtles even more, because they should always be able to get out of each other's way and must never get the feeling that they have to share their space with others. Otherwise, it can come to fierce turf wars. If you decide to keep the turtles in groups, each turtle must have enough space to retreat, so that there are no fights due to lack of space.

By Domeckopol Andreas N

Buying the Turtles

If one wants to acquire pets, many people first turn to a conventional pet shop. However, pet shops unfortunately often give the wrong advice, as staff are often not specially trained in reptiles. This is not only the case with reptiles such as turtles, but also with other popular pets such as rodents, amphibians, fish, etc. Therefore, it is advisable to take the information from pet stores with a grain of salt, to say the least.

In addition, pet stores often sell animals that are not ready to be surrendered - some animals are injured, some animals are sick, some animals are too young. It will usually be difficult for a layperson to judge whether an animal is ready to be surrendered.

Therefore, it is more advisable to buy reptiles such as turtles from a reputable breeder. Reputable breeders either focus on one specific species of turtle or on only a few different species of turtles. This allows them to gain a lot of experience and they are experts in their field.

At the time of delivery, the animals must be healthy, must not have any injuries and must be old enough. It is not necessary for a turtle to be fully grown when it is surrendered, but if it is a species of turtle that naturally holds a brumation, the first brumation should have already been completed at the breeder.

Some - not all - species of aquatic turtles hold a brumation, which is considered a survival strategy. The physical activities are reduced and the body functions are slowed down, so that the turtle can survive cold winter periods by saving energy.

Accordingly, only species that also live in the wild in areas where it is cool in the winter maintain brumation.

A reputable breeder will pay attention to all of these points and provide comprehensive advice to the new owner. Serious breeders attach great importance to the fact that their animals come into beautiful and species-appropriate homes, and therefore also gladly answer open questions. The animal will also be prepared for transport.

Of course, it is also a possibility to take over turtles from a reptile rescue station or second hand. Reptile sanctuaries are mostly privately owned and are usually not commercial enterprises. Taking over a second hand turtle because it is no longer wanted in its old home is also a commendable decision.

Nevertheless, there is the danger that one takes over unintentionally a sick animal, which would be better in expert hands at first, until it is healthy again.

The price for a turtle varies greatly depending on the species, age and sex. Worldwide, Trachemys scripta elegans are very popular because of their small size, non-aggressive nature and suitability for living in the living room at home. Moreover, they are not particularly sensitive.

However, other species are of course also extremely popular (see chapter "Popular species"). Prices for a turtle vary greatly depending on age, size, rarity, etc. For example, a juvenile of the species Trachemys scripta elegans costs between 10 dollars and 30 dollars. An adult animal costs about 30 dollars to 100 dollars.

Painted Turtles, on the other hand, usually cost 20 dollars to 50 dollars as juveniles and between 50 dollars and 200 dollars as adults.

It should be further emphasized that only offspring should be purchased as pets - preferably from a foster home or reputable breeder. Wild stocks should be left alone; also because some species of turtles are already threatened with extinction and wild captures exacerbate this.

Trachemys scripta by Sergio Cerrato

The Turtle Home

A few words in advance: for simplicity, we refer to the turtle enclosure as an "aquarium" in this book. As a rule, aquariums are purely aquatic, that is, filled with water, while terrariums have no water areas. However, an aquatic turtle enclosure has both: a large water area as well as a smaller land area. Therefore, strictly speaking, it is called an aqua-terrarium.

However, we speak of aquariums because one of the characteristics of an aquarium is the fact that it opens from the top. A terrarium, on the other hand, opens from the front, which makes terrariums useless for aquatic turtle keeping, as the water would naturally flow out. Therefore, you need an aquarium that opens from the top and can be converted to an aqua-terrarium so that the turtles always have a choice between the water and the land (for basking).

Turtles are a big responsibility! So, for most people, turtles are a lifetime commitment if they are to stay in the family forever. This is true not only for the larger species, but also for the smaller ones. It is not uncommon for even smaller species to live up to 40-50 years. So, when you buy a turtle, you are often acquiring a friend for life.

Therefore, the decision must be thoroughly thought through - and you must choose the right species for you. You also need to consider whether you can keep the turtle indoors or outdoors, because there are different species, some of which can be kept indoors or outdoors depending on the area.

Of course, whether the turtles can be kept outdoors also depends on the region in which they live. If the climate in your region roughly corresponds to the climate of the region in which the respective species is also found in nature, there is nothing against keeping them outdoors. For example, Painted Turtles (Chrysemys picta) or Red-cheeked Tortoises (Trachemys scripta elegans) are particularly popular for outdoor keeping. However, they do not have to live outdoors; they can also be housed indoors.

In general, indoor enclosures are slightly more expensive than outdoor enclosures. This is because you have to pay for UV lighting and additional equipment indoors. If you live in an area where the weather conditions (such as heat and humidity) are suitable for the tortoise species, you can keep them outdoors. But again, it depends on where you live, because a tortoise that comes from dry areas in North Africa, for example, will not tolerate high humidity, and tortoises from South America, where humidity is very high, will not cope with an environment that is too dry. Also, in many countries of Europa or the Americas (e.g., Canada), it is often too cold to keep the turtle outside year-round.

However, I would like to point out that turtles that live outdoors need to be very well protected from predators. There are many keepers and breeders who leave the turtles completely unprotected in the garden, as this is not common in all regions. However, you should keep in mind that there are many predators that can be dangerous to your animals if they are not properly protected - this also applies to other animals that live in the garden, such as rabbits, birds or guinea pigs. However, there are also predators like martens or foxes that can easily bite through ordinary fences or nets, so I would always pay the most attention to security.

Security measures should not only keep predators out, but also ensure that the turtles remain in their habitat. Remember that turtles are good at escaping. So, they should not be able to crawl under a fence or anything similar.

It is important that the turtles have both a water area and a land area available. Many keepers prefer to choose males, as females lay eggs and therefore require a bit more attention. Females need deep, fine sand to bury their eggs in. Otherwise, health problems such as egg laying may occur.

However, it is also common in groups of males that there is increased fighting and dominance behavior. There is no guarantee for this - the harmony in a group depends strongly on how the different characters get along with each other.

The aquarium should have a length of at least one meter (40 inches) if one to two animals are kept in it. For each additional animal, 20% more space should be added - for example, a length of 120 centimeters (47 inches) for three animals. The aquarium should be at least half a meter wide (20 inches). However, these are only minimum dimensions and should never be less than this - if possible, the turtles will enjoy even more space.

The water area should have a water depth of at least 40 centimeters (15 inches).

Turtles sometimes need their rest and want to retreat. You can create retreats, for example, by placing plants tactically and having decorative pieces in your aquarium.

Turtles live both on land and in water. Therefore, it is important that they can easily get from the water to land. Often it can be observed that the dry part drops down into the water. You could possibly also use some sort of stairs for the turtles to use.

The water should be kept clean at all times using an external filter, and there should be a heat lamp in the land area under which the turtles can bask at about 95°F (35°C).

Fine sand or fine gravel is particularly suitable as a substrate. The substrate layer should be approximately two to three centimeters (0.8 to 1.2 inches) high. In general, sand is more popular than gravel because it is somewhat easier to clean (for example, with a mulch bell). The material itself is the same, but sand grains are much smaller. Grains larger than two millimeters are called gravel, while grains smaller than two millimeters are called sand. If the turtles like to burrow in the sand (such as

Common Musk Turtles) the substrate can be as high as five centimeters (2 inches).

Trachemys scripta by Yavanessa Sandy Karreman

For a natural habitat, it is highly recommended to drape some aquatic plants in the aquarium. For example, the following plants are particularly suitable for a water turtle aquarium:

Elodea / Anacharis - This plant grows very quickly and is quite hardy, making it a popular aquatic plant for turtle aquariums. It provides shade, oxygenates the water and offers hiding places. Some turtles also like to eat it.

Hornwort / Anthocerotae - This plant also grows quickly, provides oxygen to the water and is quite hardy. Smaller turtle species may also use it as a hiding place.

Java Fern / Microsorum pteropus - This plant grows more slowly, but is also easy to care for. In addition, it too provides a retreat for turtles to rest.

Vallisneria - Vallisneria spiralis, Vallisneria americana as well as Vallisneria nana are especially popular in aquariums. These plants are very hardy and are suitable for a wide range of aquariums. There are fourteen different species that are widely used in freshwater or brackish water in the tropics and subtropics.

A UVB lamp should never be missing. Although no lamp can replace real sun, it should always be available for turtles kept indoors. There are UVB lamps that are specially made and adapted for reptiles, because other exotic animals such as bearded dragons or geckos also need additional irradiation - both as a light source and as a heat source. (Example: Zoo Med brand Power Sun UV lamp; I am not affiliated with this company and am not paid to promote this company; this is an example and there are many other suitable lamps).

It is also imperative that the turtle enclosure be equipped with a thermometer and a hygrometer. The thermometer is used to measure temperature, while the hygrometer is used to measure humidity. Both are important. Nowadays, there are often devices that combine both thermometer and hygrometer in one unit.

Since most species of turtles kept as pets come from rather warm regions, care must always be taken to ensure that the enclosure is warm enough. Of course, this also depends on what region you live in, but many of the readers of this book will come from areas where it is quite cold at least some of the time, such as the northern countries of Europa, North America, etc.

Therefore, the living conditions from the home country of the particular species of turtle must be replicated as closely as possible - otherwise the animal may become ill because, for example, its metabolism slows down considerably.

Emys orbicularis by Onkel Ramirez

The Diet

Most aquatic turtles are omnivores. Animals are divided into three broad categories based on their different diets: Carnivores (carnivores), Omnivores (omnivores), and Herbivores (herbivores). Within these head categories there may be further special subdivisions; for example, insectivores (insect eaters) belong to the carnivore category.

While land turtles are to a very large extent herbivores, most aquatic turtles are omnivores and feed on both animal and plant foods.

Aquatic turtles should always be fed in the water rather than on land, as they need water to swallow the food.

They are very greedy and in captivity they usually do not regulate their food intake themselves, but always ask for more food. Humans have a responsibility in this regard to ensure that the animals do not become too fat and are fed a healthy, varied diet.

Turtles are cold-blooded animals and, unlike us humans, do not need food to maintain their body temperature. They use the energy they consume just to grow and move around. So the amount of food you should give your turtle depends on its size, age, activity level and also the species. You should only give turtles as much food as they can eat in about five minutes.

Young turtles grow faster and therefore need more food than older animals. The best type of food to give your animal also depends on its age.

All tortoises should be given fresh vegetable food daily. Animal food depends on age - if the turtle is younger than six months, it should be given animal food daily. If the turtle is between six months and two years old, it should receive animal food every two days. For tortoises older than two years, it is enough to give them animal food twice a week.

If a turtle is too fat, a fasting day will not hurt either. It is advisable to weigh the animals about once a week and record the weight. It is best to feed your turtle in the morning. Just like humans, turtles can digest their food better during the day.

Industrial ready-made food is commonly found in stores, but this is obviously not the ideal diet for turtles. I advise feeding only fresh food, as this is the most species-appropriate and ensures a long, healthy life.

Industrially produced ready-made food does not contain all the necessary interacting substances and vitamins. This type of food may be suitable as a supplementary food for young turtles. However, do not forget to give your animal other food as well.

Not all species of aquatic turtles eat animal and plant foods in the same proportion. For example, a red-cheeked slider turtle's diet consists of over 80% plant food. In addition, the amount of meat you can give your turtle also depends on its age and behavior. While young turtles' diet consists of 90% animal foods, older animals only need 50%.

Also, you should not feed aggressive turtles too much meat. You can choose between live food and dead food. You can buy live food animals (crickets, grasshoppers, worms and the like) in a store or order them online. Stream fleas are especially popular!

Even with plant foods, the "what" and "how much" depends on the type of turtle. Yellow-cheeked and yellow-bellied turtles, for example, will not eat fruit.

However, for most species, the following rule applies: the older the animal, the more plant food it needs. You will find that your turtle will nibble on the plants in its water. Therefore, never use poisonous plants. You can give your turtle leafy vegetables, for example.

However, it is important to say that the feeding of iceberg lettuce and lettuce is already outdated in many countries. These types of lettuce have a lot of nitrate and provide very little nutrients and crude fiber, so they are neither particularly nutritious for the turtle and can even cause diarrhea due to the high nitrate content.

Suitable lettuces are, for example:

- Kale

- romaine lettuce

- radicchio

- Lamb's lettuce

- rocket

However, it is even better if you can offer the turtles fresh wild herbs, for example, from your own garden or from a forest. This is not only extremely inexpensive, but also very healthy. The following wild herbs are especially good:

- Dandelion (both the leaves and the flowers)
- Daisies

- Clover

- Thistles

- Ribwort and plantain

- Chickweed

- Cranesbill

- Alfalfa

- Speedwell

A fantastic food for turtles is Golliwoog. Golliwoog is a fast-growing plant that is readily eaten by many reptiles, as well as birds and rodents, because it provides many important vitamins and minerals. The ratio of phosphorus and calcium in Golliwoog is optimal for turtles. In addition, Golliwoog is also known as "creeping beautiful cushion" because it spreads wherever it can grow creeping on the ground. Golliwoog is considered a weed in many countries, but is particularly nutritious (similar to dandelions, which are also often undesirable, but make an excellent weed to feed on). The scientific name of golliwoog is Callisia repens.

Emys orbicularis by Onkel Ramirez

Some plants are toxic to turtles. A well-known example is ivy.

In addition, it is essential to make sure that the turtle's bones and shell stay nice and strong. Especially during growth this is very important so that no diseases develop and so that the young turtle can grow well, but also for adult animals this is of utmost relevance for strong and stable bones and a strong stable shell. For this reason, turtles should always have access to cuttlebone or algal lime. But why is this so?

In the wild, animals can specifically seek out food that meets their nutritional needs. For example, they sometimes find sources of various minerals on the ground. Furthermore, animals in the wild get enough vitamin D3 - which is strictly speaking a hormone, but is called a vitamin - through direct sunlight on the body. In the enclosure, this is limited if, for example, special UVB fluorescent tubes are used.

Calcium is an extremely important mineral for turtles that almost always needs to be supplemented. Failure to do so could result in calcium deficiency (hypocalcemia) or the animals could develop rickets (bone disease; soft and/or bent bones).

Since calcium is so important for the bones and for the shell, among other things for their construction and stability, calcium should always be freely available to the turtles. Often a small bowl of calcium powder is permanently offered to the animals in the enclosure. Especially juveniles and pregnant females need this for healthy growth and/or egg production, but adult turtles are also strongly dependent on an adequate calcium supply.

A majority of breeders and owners resort to the cuttlebone powder (or crushed cuttlebone shells) for calcium supply. This comes from the cuttlefish and in most cases smells accordingly strong.

Aquatic turtles eat insects in their natural environment and these are used as part of their diet. But which animal feeds are suitable?

- Brown shrimps

- crickets

- grasshoppers

- worms

- mealworms

- wax worms

- snails

- possibly fish

In addition to leafy green vegetables such as salads, herbs and insects, the diet can also be supplemented with a bit of vegetables, for example:

- Carrots

- pumpkin

- peas

- celery

- chicory

Even if you are in good health and not overweight, it is recommended to have a fasting day every now and then. Regular fasting days can help turtles relieve stress on their digestive tract. One to two fasting days per week are completely safe for healthy turtles and are even helpful in maintaining good long-term health.

By Christel Chiem Seherin

Brumation

Some species of aquatic turtles go into dormancy during the cold months, when they go into what is called brumation. This does not apply to all species, however, as it depends greatly on the region from which the particular turtle originated.

The animals go into brumation because they can find no or hardly any food in their natural environment during the winter months and because, in addition, it is too cold for the animals during the winter months - because reptiles cannot regulate their body temperature themselves (unlike mammals), but the body temperature depends on the ambient temperature.

For this reason, turtle species that come from regions where it is warm all year round do not need to rest during the winter months and do not require brumation. The situation is different for species that originate from cooler countries where it is warm in the summer and very cold in the winter. In brumation, basic body functions are maintained, but the entire metabolism is very much shut down. The body has time to regenerate and recover.

Brumation should be distinguished from hibernation. Some mammals keep a strict hibernation, during which they actually sleep deeply and shut down completely in the long run. Brumation differs from this because the aquatic turtle does not sleep completely and continuously, but instead exhibits very reduced activity - it just comes to rest for a time and "freezes". During brumation, the metabolism is shut down and the heart beats more slowly.

Some species initiate brumation on their own when light conditions get darker and the temperature gets cooler. Slowly, they eat less, become quieter, and are generally less active. Brumation begins when the days get shorter, temperatures decrease, and it slowly gets darker. Usually, brumation is initiated in October or November. Animals often sense the right time themselves and they usually stop eating on their own - the owner should not deprive them of food.

Also, it is often advised to give the turtle a warm bath several times before brumation so that the intestines empty completely. This is not advisable as there are examples where the tortoise has starved to death during brumation. Metabolism is greatly reduced, but the animals still need access to nutrients.

It is a good idea to weigh a tortoise in brumation about once a month. Small fluctuations in weight are normal, but if there is a weight loss of more than 10%, something is wrong. The animal is breaking down too much (possibly due to an overlooked parasite infestation) and should be taken out of brumation early before it starves to death or suffers other further damage to its health.

However, it is important that only healthy tortoises are "sent" into brumation. Sick animals should not be held in brumation. Sometimes illnesses are not immediately apparent, so the tortoise should be examined for general health and parasites before beginning brumation. At a minimum, a fecal sample should be examined for this purpose. If parasites are detected, the animal should not go into brumation, because this can cause the parasites to multiply even more and radically worsen the situation!

At the beginning of the brumation the feeding of the turtles is reduced. This lends itself to the period from early October to early November, and often the turtle initiates this on its own. The turtle then excretes the food remains that are still in its body.

The problem with this, however, is that most tortoises kept as pets do not live outdoors, but in a domestic enclosure where the temperature, light and humidity are regulated by humans. Therefore, they often do not get to see how the weather changes outside the door, and the natural introduction is difficult. Here, humans help to gradually replicate the natural developments.

About two to three weeks after the last feeding, the turtles go into brumation. This is the time the tortoise needs to empty its bowels - at the onset of brumation, the bowels should not be full, but they should not be completely empty either (hence no warm baths).

Prior to this, the heat in the enclosure is gradually turned down - at what intervals this should be done is not strictly prescribed, as of course the temperature in the natural environment also changes quite slowly.

The subsequent brumation should be maintained at a temperature of a constant four to six degrees Celsius (39-43°F). In some areas, it is a good idea to move the turtle to the cool basement. If the cold temperatures cannot be guaranteed, it is a good idea to acquire a separate small refrigerator in which the temperature can be very well controlled and which is regularly ventilated to provide oxygen.

During brumation, the turtle is kept in a plastic container with water. The turtle should have the opportunity to breathe at all times, but the water should reach the shell to prevent the animal from drying out. Most keepers perform hibernation over a period of about three months.

However, it should not be warmer than four to six degrees Celsius (39-43°F) and the temperature must be kept well in mind, since the metabolism already starts up again at about 8°C (46°F) and the turtle begins to break down fat. Thus, temperatures that are too "warm" can be life-threatening.

After brumation, it is important that the tortoise be re-acclimated to warmer temperatures and more light only slowly. The lighting duration is slowly increased and the temperatures or water temperatures slowly become warmer.

Chrysemys picta - By Dan Thomas Wildernessman

Common Diseases

Everyone gets sick sometimes. Some more often, others less often. Even reptiles like aquatic turtles do not avoid diseases and the severity ranges from "mild" to "potentially fatal". But how often and how severely an aquatic turtle gets sick is largely something you can help determine. As with humans, prevention is key - an aquatic turtle that is kept in a species-appropriate manner, whose needs are met, and which receives a balanced and healthy diet, is very unlikely to become ill.

Of course, certain diseases can occur even if an animal is kept in perfect conditions, such as through heredity or just plain bad luck. However, over 90% of diseases in reptiles are caused by humans - not intentionally, but the majority by simple ignorance regarding optimal husbandry conditions.

Among the most common mistakes in terms of husbandry and nutrition are, for example ...

... too little water, too little air humidity

... overfeeding (many species in "captivity" often gratefully accept everything that humans provide and often no longer regulate themselves)

... no brumation (for species that keep brumation in nature; does not apply to all species)

... stress (e.g. due to lack of space and/or wrong group constellations)

... fear

... too high or too low temperatures

It is not always necessary to visit the vet for every little thing. A visit to the vet is always connected with stress, because the water turtle is torn from its usual environment and must face a very stressful and exhausting situation for it, which can sometimes even take several hours including travel.

Nevertheless, for liability reasons I will not recommend self-treatment and self-medication. Especially beginners may misjudge diseases and treat them wrongly, because they do not have much experience with aquatic turtles. Accordingly, I would like to point out that diseases must always be identified and professionally treated by an expert veterinarian.

When choosing a veterinarian, make sure that the person selected has experience with reptiles. This is an absolute must. Reptiles are so fundamentally different from other pets such as rodents, dogs, cats, etc. that a reptile cannot be treated by just any veterinarian. In any case, a reputable veterinarian will only treat a water turtle if they feel confident to do so based on their experience and can treat the animal professionally.

In some areas, it can be quite difficult to find a veterinarian who is well versed in reptiles. This varies from region to region. It is possible that quite a long journey must be accepted. A long journey is of course associated with more stress for the animal, but this is better than if the animal would be treated by a veterinarian who is not well versed in reptiles and may make mistakes. Therefore, it is advisable to start looking for a suitable veterinarian at an early stage in order to have the right contact person at hand immediately in case of an emergency.

Of course, the owner must be sensitized to the recognition of diseases. If you know your animals, you will notice it quite quickly if something is wrong and if an animal changes. Not every little change has to be a sign of a disease, but the following signs often indicate diseases - especially if they occur in a combination ...

... loss of appetite, refusal of food

... sudden aggressiveness and irritability; or the opposite: sudden lethargy / apathy

... unnatural movement patterns

... changes in excretions (feces and urine) in terms of shape, color and/or consistency

... loss of the joy of movement

... discoloration or detachment of the skin

Although a disease is a case for the vet, the owner should be able to recognize the different diseases in principle. Therefore, we will now take a closer look at some common aquatic turtle diseases.

- Abscesses and possibly sepsis

Abscesses are accumulations of pus, which are caused by bacteria. In principle, an abscess can occur on any part of the body. As a rule, an abscess is caused by an external injury, for example by a cut on a sharp object. Bacteria can now enter the animal's body through the open wound and possibly cause an infectious abscess.

When reptiles get an abscess, however, the pus in this is usually not liquid, but encapsulated and quite hard. In the worst case, the bursting of the abscess can lead to blood poisoning (sepsis) if the germs enter the bloodstream through this, and the animal may even die. Therefore, many abscesses must be surgically removed. Whether surgery is necessary and what treatment is appropriate will be decided by the knowledgeable veterinarian.

The most common abscess in aquatic turtles is ear abscess (otitis media). The bump is usually very clearly visible. Here said bacteria have not entered the body through, for example, a wound, but through the ear; the germs have ascended through the ear canal into the middle ear. This is usually caused by poor hygiene, but also by drafts, for example.

- Intestinal parasites

Parasites are basically divided into ectoparasites and endoparasites. Ectoparasites are "external living" parasites, for example mites on the skin, but ectoparasites like mites or ticks are very rare in aquatic turtles. Endoparasites are "internal living" parasites. Intestinal parasites are therefore classified as endoparasites. They include, for example, tapeworms, hexamites and the like. Almost all animals are sooner or later infested by parasites and this is usually easily treatable.

However, in artificially created habitats - for example, in enclosures of aquatic turtles - an infestation increases quite quickly if it is not detected and treated early, because there is not too much space available in the enclosure. How strong or weak the parasite infestation is often also strongly depends on the animal's psyche. Stress, fear and other negative emotions weaken the animal's immune system and thus its defenses.

If an animal is infested with intestinal parasites, this can usually be recognized quite easily from the feces. The consistency of the feces becomes soft and resembles mush, and in acute infestation, severe diarrhea often occurs as well. In addition, the diseased animal often loses weight (sometimes rapidly) and even with good nutrition.

By Ralphs_Fotos

- Diarrhea

As we have previously noted, intestinal parasites can cause diarrhea. However, diarrhea is not due to parasite infestation in all cases. There are many possible reasons for diarrhea. Because diarrhea can sometimes cause an animal to become dehydrated or dehydrated very quickly, it is important to identify the cause of the fecal change.

Dehydration of the body also causes kidney dysfunction, electrolyte loss, and can lead to other diseases. Diarrhea is defined as not only watery feces, but also mucous and very soft feces. Particularly urgent action is required if there is even blood in the feces. An expert veterinarian must be consulted immediately.

In addition to intestinal parasites, the following factors can also cause diarrhea ...

... stress and other psychological strains

... spoiled food

... foreign food

... a lot of fruit / sugar

... a too fast change of the food

... overfeeding or malnutrition

... medication

... diseases of the liver or gall bladder

... toxins

- Moulting problems

As reptiles grow throughout their lives, they shed their skin regularly. A healthy and species-appropriate aquatic turtle has no problems with molting and does it without complications. However, if an animal has molting problems, the molt either fails completely or certain parts of the skin do not detach from the body. In most cases, molting problems are due to insufficient humidity in the enclosure. In some cases, conditions that are too dry make molting incredibly difficult.

Other conditions such as dehydration or infection can also complicate molting. Unlike some other reptiles such as snakes, turtles do not shed their skin in its entirety, but the skin is continuously renewed, so it is often hardly noticeable (unlike a snake). More often, for example, skin fragments are discovered in the neck area or on the limbs.

Particularly important for molting aquatic turtles are abrasion opportunities underwater (for example, large rocks) and a warm basking spot (usually 35°C (95°F)).

Vitamin A deficiency can also lead to molting problems.

- Liver Diseases

Liver disease is quite common in reptiles when the liver is permanently overworked due to improper husbandry conditions. The liver is a detoxification organ and also needs a break every now and then. An unhealthy lifestyle puts too much strain on the liver and it cannot recover from its work. Therefore, liver disease is usually caused when an animal is fed too often on a permanent basis and/or is fed food that is too high in calories.

People sometimes mean too well for the animal and overfeed it. However, this is detrimental to health, as aquatic turtles simply have a different feeding rhythm than, for example, humans or other popular pets.

Also, a lack of brumation can feel if necessary to liver diseases or diseases of other organs, because during brumation the body has a lot of time to recover and regenerate. Liver diseases develop rather slowly, so at first there are usually no symptoms. At a later stage, the urine and feces of the diseased animal often become discolored and take on an unnatural coloration. To relieve the liver, kidneys and intestines, it is therefore recommended to establish one or two fasting days per week.

- Egg binding

When females have problems laying eggs, this is called egg binding. The eggs may either not be laid at all or only partially, they may block the cloaca and/or fallopian tube, cause prolapse (prolapse) and in the worst case may even rot in the animal's body.

In acute egg binding, which is not treated in time, the animal may even die - for example, from blood poisoning or kidney failure.

The blockages can cause bloating, cramps, refusal to eat and the like. Egg binding can occur, for example, when a female is kept in unnatural conditions. However, egg binding can also occur if there are no suitable places for egg laying. In addition, deficiency symptoms such as vitamin D3 deficiency are often a reason for egg binding. In order to prevent egg binding, a sufficient supply of all necessary vitamins and minerals should be ensured. Also egg laying places should not be missing. If egg binding still occurs, a veterinarian experienced in reptiles should be consulted quickly. Egg binding often leads to paralysis of the hind legs and restless behavior.

- Mouth rot (Stomatitis)

Mouth rot (stomatitis) involves infections in the mouth of the animal. Stomatitis is usually more common in snakes than in turtles or lizards. Stomatitis often develops as a result of other infections in the body or parasite infestation. General metabolic disorders can also trigger the condition. If the oral mucosa is injured, stomatitis has an easy time. If there is also a wound in the mouth, this can also lead to a bacterial infection of the same. In the worst case, stomatitis can even cause blood poisoning and abscesses can form. The diseased animal often dehydrates quite quickly and often refuses food. The following two points are particularly important to note:

1. stomatitis occurs most often in aquatic turtles after brumation! (If it is a species that holds a brumation).

2. stomatitis can be a sign of herpes in turtles - and this infection is especially dangerous for turtles!

- Kidney diseases

Kidney disease, much like liver disease, is quite common in reptiles. Much like the liver, the kidneys take care of detoxifying the body. The kidneys function like a toxin filter for the body, and they drain out germs and other pathogens. If the kidneys are diseased, the urine is usually discolored, too dark, somewhat slimy or too cloudy. Like liver disease, kidney disease tends to develop slowly and insidiously, but it is almost always triggered by improper housing conditions. For healthy kidneys, adequate fluid intake is key. If an animal is dehydrated or takes in too little water, this can lead to sometimes severe damage to the kidneys in the long term. However, hypothermia can also lead to kidney damage over time. Therefore, appropriate temperatures must always be maintained. Important: In case of green urine, a veterinarian must be consulted immediately! Green urine is a sign of kidney failure and/or a very heavy parasite infestation.

By Ralphs_Fotos

- Rickets

Rickets is also often referred to as metabolic bone disease. It is a disease of the bones caused by a permanent calcium deficiency. Calcium deficiency is also known as hypocalcemia. Adequate calcium intake - in combination with vitamins D3 and K and with magnesium - is essential and absolutely necessary for healthy and stable bones and a healthy and stable carapace.

In rickets, there is decreased bone density and a change in bone composition. Especially young animals and pregnant females have an increased need for the previously mentioned micronutrients. Damage is usually very difficult or impossible to heal. If an animal has rickets, the bones become soft, and they deform. Deformities may occur and the bones may thicken in certain areas.

Consequential diseases can be triggered by rickets, because the diseased animal often has limitations of the musculoskeletal system, suffers from calcifications and kidney diseases, sometimes has problems with food intake due to deformed jaws and much more. Egg binding can also occur in females. Therefore, it is important to prevent rickets from occurring in the first place - by providing sufficient essential micronutrients.

- Herpes infection

Herpes infections are among the most serious diseases a turtle can contract. Among turtles, herpes is considered a plague and once the virus is transmitted to a turtle, it is irreversible - the turtle will carry the virus throughout its life and may transmit it to other animals. For groups, therefore, it is important to ensure that any new addition is not a carrier of the herpes virus under any circumstances and regular blood tests should be performed. This does not mean that the turtle has to die from the outbreak of the herpes virus, but it will carry the virus throughout its life, it can pass it on and it can come to new outbreaks of the disease. Especially in stressful situations there is an increased outbreak of the disease, for example because stress has been shown to weaken the immune system. In addition, it also depends on the respective type of turtle - commonly, however, tortoises are considered more susceptible to herpes diseases than aquatic turtles or terrapins. However, this is only a tendency and it depends heavily on the health or defenses of the particular turtle.

Before we look at the symptoms for a herpes infection, however, it should be said that it is also possible for a turtle to die suddenly without any prior signs of illness. While this is not common, it is possible.

Symptoms include, for example:

- Discomfort when swallowing or paralysis of swallowing.

- Yellowish tongue coating

- Shortness of breath

- Loss of appetite and apathy, even unconsciousness

- Unnatural movements

- Mucous secretions (from the nose or throat)

- Colds:

Turtles can catch colds too! Symptoms include the common cold symptoms such as labored breathing, mucus in the nose and/or mouth, noisy breathing, red eyes, watery eyes or dried secretions, loss of appetite, etc. Often colds are triggered by temperatures that are too cool, but also by drafts. A weakened immune system due to stress and/or a diet that does not cover all nutrients do the rest.

As with all other diseases, a competent veterinarian specializing in reptiles will decide how treatments will be given. In severe cases, the administration of antibiotics is also a possibility.

- Necrosis of the carapace; carapace necrosis.

In this disease, a white-yellowish coating can be seen on the shell of the turtle. Under this coating there are wounds in the carapace. Often this disease results from bacterial infection and/or poor hygiene. Usually, the necrosis is treated by means of an ointment that a knowledgeable veterinarian will prescribe.

To allow the ointment to take effect, the diseased turtle should be separated and kept dry for half a day. Irradiation with UV light has a supporting effect.

- Vitamin A deficiency

Vitamin A deficiency is unfortunately common in tortoises if they are not fed a varied diet. As a result of this deficiency, for example, white spot disease, eye problems or even blindness can occur. Carrots and earthworms, for example, are especially rich in vitamin A. In general, attention should always be paid to a varied diet, both in terms of plant and animal foods.

Trachemys scripta by Dezalb

Frequently Asked Questions

How old is the oldest pet aquatic turtle?

The oldest pet aquatic turtle is 56 years old. However, it is not uncommon for aquatic turtles to live up to 40-50 years if properly cared for, fed appropriately, and kept in a healthy environment.

Can I keep sea turtles as pets?

Yes, sea turtles can be kept as pets. However, it should be noted that they require special care, including a large aquarium with a controlled saltwater environment and a diet of live or frozen seafood. Keeping saltwater turtles can be a demanding and expensive hobby. Therefore, it is important to be well informed and understand their needs before acquiring a turtle as a pet.

That's why we've focused on freshwater turtle conservation in this book.

What water can I use for aquatic?

For aquatic turtles as pets, I recommend using dechlorinated tap water or bottled spring water for their aquarium. Avoid distilled water or reverse osmosis water as they do not contain the minerals and electrolytes aquatic turtles need.

You can also use a water purifier to remove harmful chemicals and restore the proper pH balance for the turtle. It is also important to maintain water quality and perform partial water changes regularly to keep the water fresh and clean. An external filter is also recommended.

Is the aquatic turtle's shell part of the body or is it a separate shell?

The shell of a turtle is its exoskeleton. The exoskeleton is a hard outer shell that protects the animal's body and supports its muscles and internal organs - so it is an external skeleton! We humans have only an internal skeleton. A turtle's shell is made of bones covered with scales, hard, protective layers of keratin. The shell protects the turtle and helps it regulate its body temperature. It also allows the turtle to hide and make itself very small.

How do aquatic turtles breathe? Do they have gills or lungs?

Aquatic turtles, like humans and other mammals, breathe air through their lungs. They have a lung system similar to that of birds and reptiles that allows them to extract oxygen from the air. Turtles can also extract oxygen from water through special structures in their mouths and throats, but they still need air to breathe. It is important that the turtle has enough surface area in the aquarium to come to the surface and breathe air. Therefore, it is important that there is also a land area where the turtle can rest and bask.

How long can an aquatic turtle stay underwater before it needs to come to the surface to breathe?

How long a turtle can stay underwater before it needs to come to the surface to breathe depends on a number of factors, including the species, size, age and health of the turtle, as well as the water temperature and oxygen content of the water.

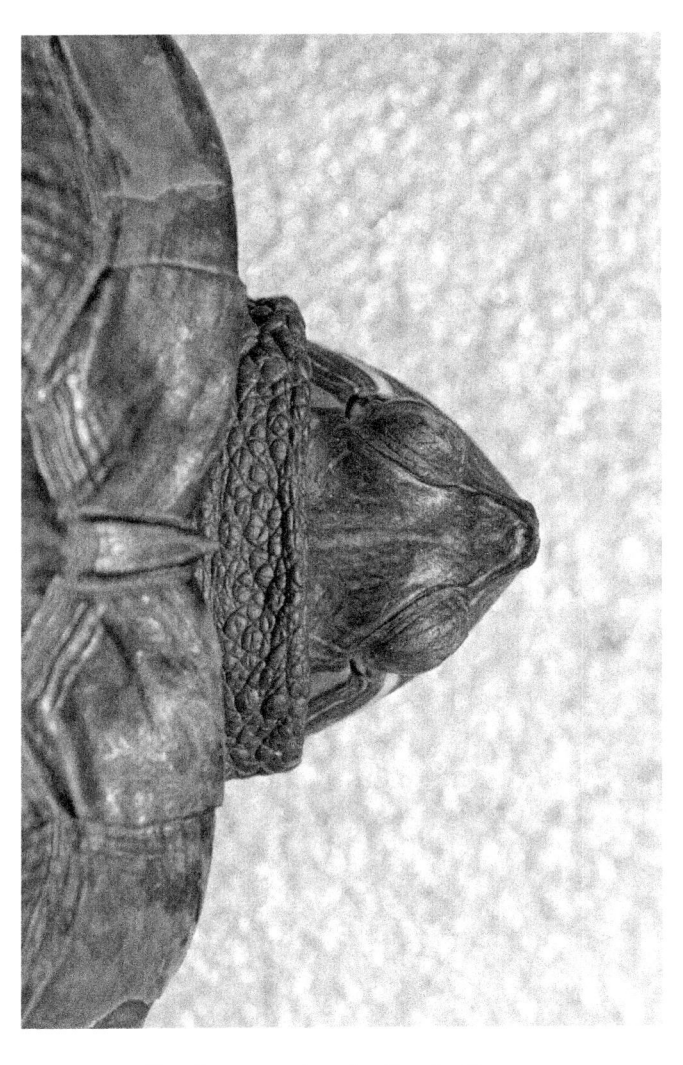

Trachemys scripta by Sergio Cerrato

On average, most aquatic turtles can remain underwater for 20 to 60 minutes before they need to breathe.

However, some species, such as the Common Musk Turtle, can stay underwater much longer. It is important that the turtle have adequate access to air. Therefore, the water area should be about 40 inches high, but leave enough room for the land area so the turtle can rest, lounge and breathe on land.

How often should I change the water in my aquarium?

We recommend doing a partial water change of about 20-45% of the water volume once a week. This will maintain good water quality and remove waste and detritus. An external filter will also clean the water.

What pH value should the water have?

A pH between 7.0 and 8.0 is suitable for aquatic turtles. It is important to maintain this pH because it is nearly neutral and helps prevent health problems in turtles. However, the ideal pH may vary slightly depending on the species of turtle.

An example for Painted Turtles:

pH: 6 to 8.5

Nitrite: Nitrite is very toxic and should not be detectable in water analysis.

Nitrate: less than 100 mg/l, ideally less than 50 mg/l.

Ammonia: less than 0.5 mg/l.

Phosphate: less than 0.5 mg/l, up to 1.5 mg/l is also acceptable.

Which turtles are best to keep as pets?

This varies somewhat from country to country. In Germany, for example, the European Pond Turtle (Emys orbicularis) is one of the most popular aquatic turtles to keep as a pet. Among other countries, it originates from Germany and is often kept in aquariums. In addition, other species such as the red ornate turtle are also very popular.

In the USA, the red-cheeked ornamental turtle is at the top of the popularity scale. By the way, it originates from the USA and can be kept both indoors and in the garden. But Painted Turtles also occupy the top ranks of the popularity scale in both countries.

In the United Kingdom and France, the red-cheeked turtle is also the most popular turtle.

Why is it necessary to warm the aquarium?

Reptiles and amphibians are cold-blooded animals. In nature, reptiles and amphibians need the warmth of the sun to warm up. Lamps and/or heaters can be used to keep them warm enough in a shelter. Heat makes animals active and triggers processes in their bodies. The supply of heat is therefore crucial for the health of the animal.

Trachemys scripta by Svetlana Zoosnow

Legal Notice

This book is protected by copyright. Reproduction by third parties is prohibited. Use or distribution by unauthorized third parties in any printed, audiovisual, audio or other media is prohibited. All rights remain solely with the author.

Author: Alina Daria Djavidrad

Contact: Wahlerstraße 1, 40472 Düsseldorf, Germany.

© 2023 Alina Daria Djavidrad

First edition (2023)

Trachemys scripta by Yavanessa Sandy Karreman

By Ralphs_Fotos

Dear Readers

For independent authors, product reviews are the foundation of a book's success. That is why we depend on your reviews.

This helps not only the authors, but of course also future readers and especially the animals!

Therefore, I should be grateful for a little review on this book. Thank you so much for your support!

I wish you all the best, much joy with your pets and stay healthy!

Room for Notes

Printed in Great Britain
by Amazon